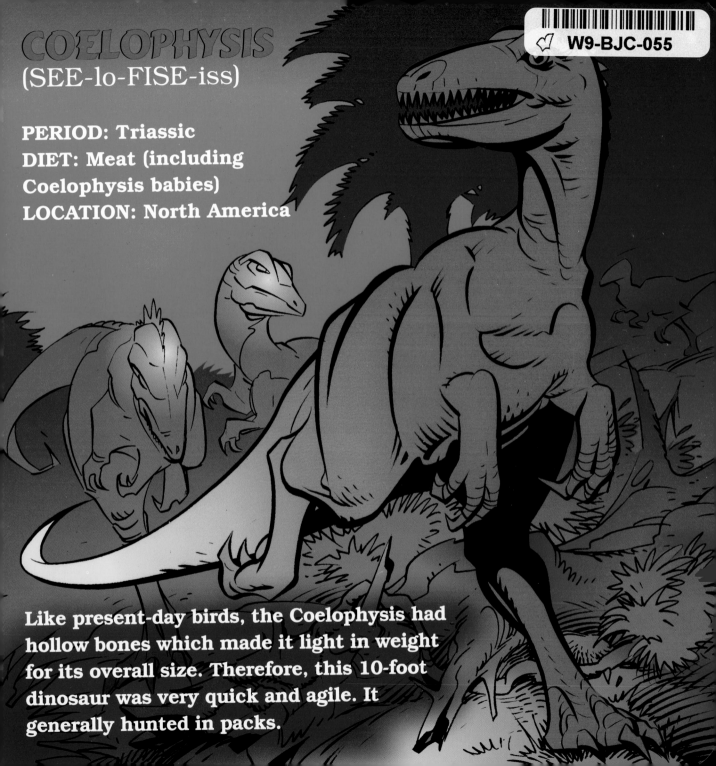

COELOPHYSIS
(SEE-lo-FISE-iss)

PERIOD: Triassic
DIET: Meat (including Coelophysis babies)
LOCATION: North America

Like present-day birds, the Coelophysis had hollow bones which made it light in weight for its overall size. Therefore, this 10-foot dinosaur was very quick and agile. It generally hunted in packs.

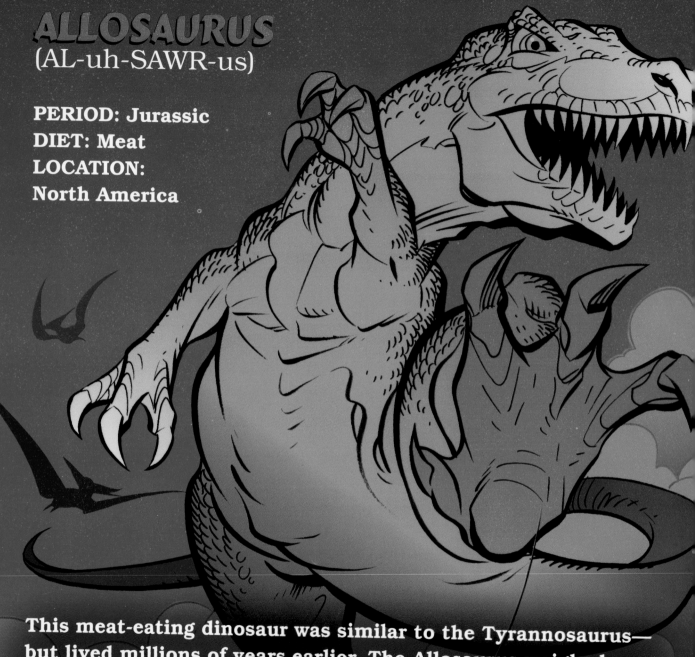

ALLOSAURUS
(AL-uh-SAWR-us)

PERIOD: Jurassic
DIET: Meat
LOCATION:
North America

This meat-eating dinosaur was similar to the Tyrannosaurus—but lived millions of years earlier. The Allosaurus weighed about 2 tons and hunted dinosaurs even larger than itself, possibly even the 100-ton Apatosaurus!

STEGOSAURUS
(STEG-uh-SAWR-us)

PERIOD: Jurassic
DIET: Plants
LOCATION: North America

With long, sharp spikes on its thick tail and pointed bony plates on its back, the Stegosaurus was well prepared to defend itself against dinosaur attack.

BRACHIOSAURUS
(BRAK-ee-uh-SAWR-us)

PERIOD: Jurassic

DIET: Plants

LOCATION: North America and East Africa

Weighing up to 100 tons and measuring almost 100 feet in length, the Brachiosaurus was one of the biggest dinosaurs ever! Using its long neck, it could feast on the leaves of the tallest trees.

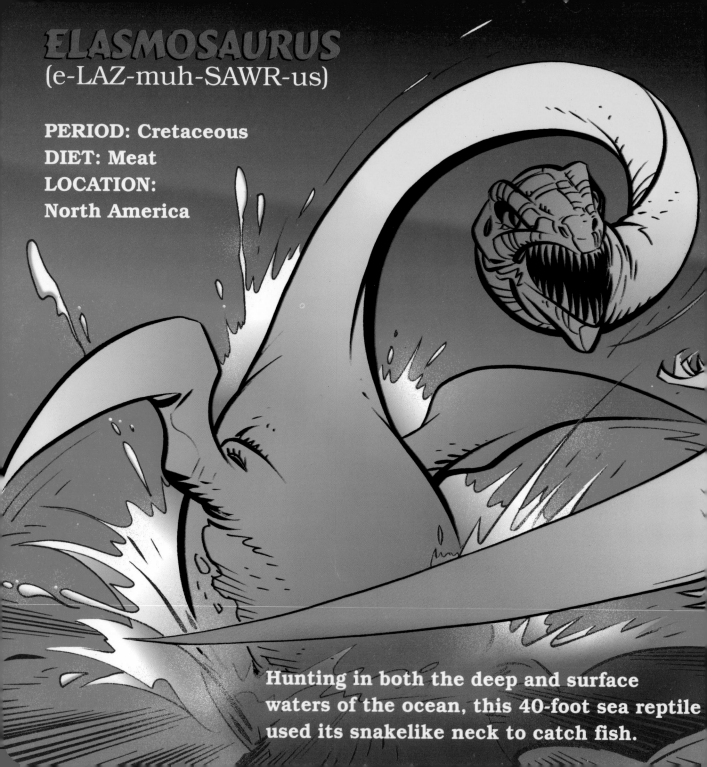

ELASMOSAURUS
(e-LAZ-muh-SAWR-us)

PERIOD: Cretaceous
DIET: Meat
LOCATION:
North America

Hunting in both the deep and surface waters of the ocean, this 40-foot sea reptile used its snakelike neck to catch fish.

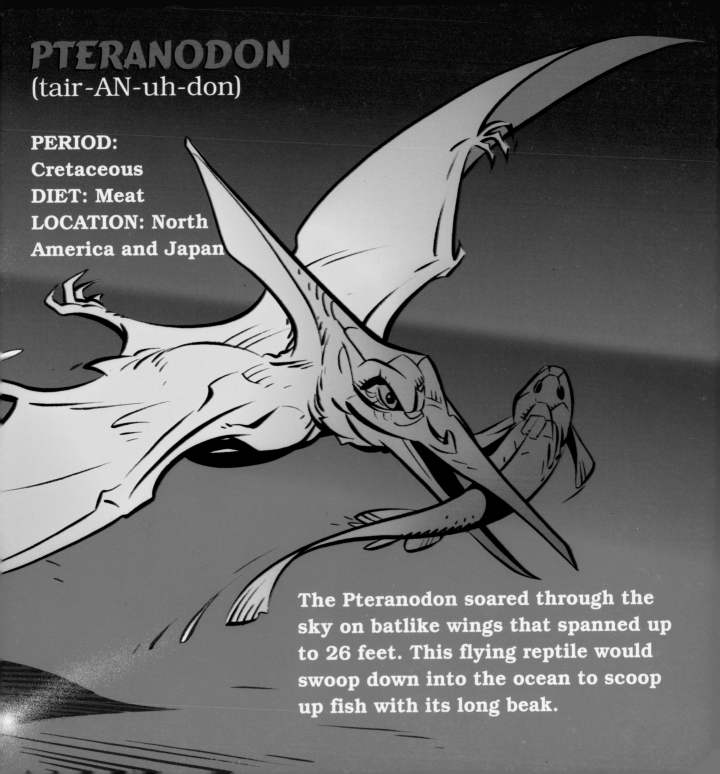

PTERANODON
(tair-AN-uh-don)

PERIOD:
Cretaceous
DIET: Meat
LOCATION: North
America and Japan

The Pteranodon soared through the sky on batlike wings that spanned up to 26 feet. This flying reptile would swoop down into the ocean to scoop up fish with its long beak.

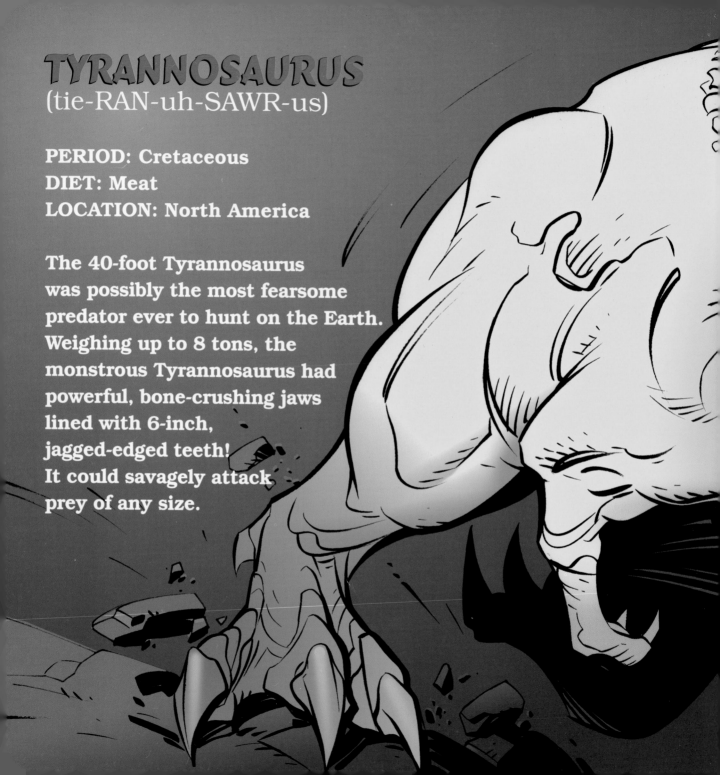

TYRANNOSAURUS
(tie-RAN-uh-SAWR-us)

PERIOD: Cretaceous
DIET: Meat
LOCATION: North America

The 40-foot Tyrannosaurus was possibly the most fearsome predator ever to hunt on the Earth. Weighing up to 8 tons, the monstrous Tyrannosaurus had powerful, bone-crushing jaws lined with 6-inch, jagged-edged teeth! It could savagely attack prey of any size.

TRICERATOPS
(try-SAIR-uh-TOPS)

PERIOD: Cretaceous
DIET: Plants
LOCATION: North America

This 6-ton, tanklike dinosaur had sharp horns and a bony neck frill to ward off attacks. When confronted by dinosaurs such as the Tyrannosaurus, the Triceratops would charge at the predator's unprotected belly.

SPINOSAURUS
(SPY-nuh-SAWR-us)

PERIOD: Cretaceous
DIET: Meat
LOCATION: Africa

Some of the spines that gave this predator its name could grow up to 6 feet in height. The bony fin made by these spines may have been used by the Spinosaurus to regulate its body temperature as well as for defense.

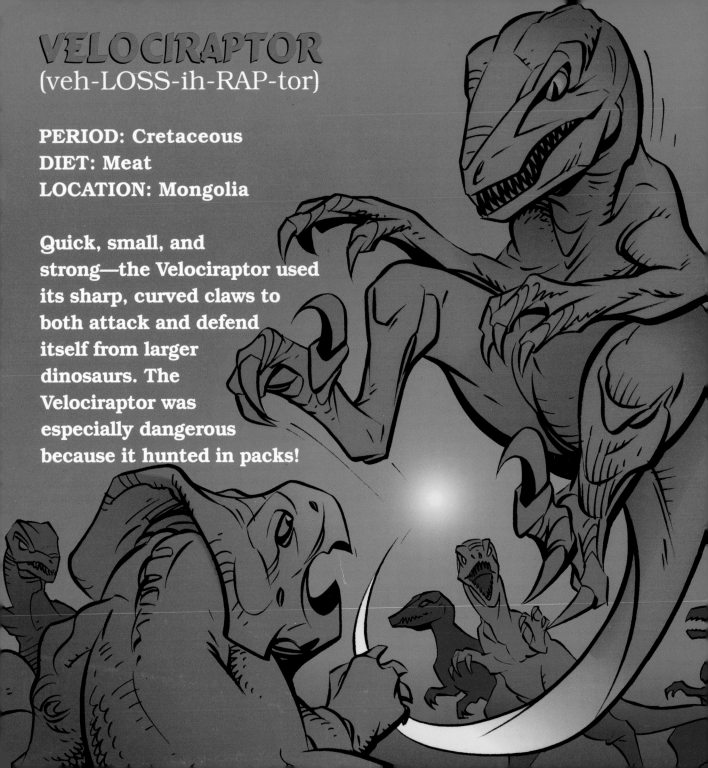

VELOCIRAPTOR
(veh-LOSS-ih-RAP-tor)

PERIOD: Cretaceous
DIET: Meat
LOCATION: Mongolia

Quick, small, and strong—the Velociraptor used its sharp, curved claws to both attack and defend itself from larger dinosaurs. The Velociraptor was especially dangerous because it hunted in packs!

THE END OF THE DINOSAURS

Dinosaurs died out about 65 million years ago. Today the skeletons and fossils displayed in museums are all that remain of these monsters that once ruled the Earth.

SCREAMIN' 3-D GLASSES INSIDE!™

Discover Screamin' 3-D—and discover dinosaurs that rip, tear, and bite their way off each page! A startling new 3-D process will unleash the prehistoric giants right before your eyes.

By Dennis R. Shealy

Illustrated by Ken Steacy

Books in this series:
Dr. Skincrawl's Creepy Creatures
Night for a Fairy Ball
Dinosaurs
Food Fright
Boo Goes There?

A GOLDEN BOOK • NEW YORK

Golden Books Publishing Company, Inc.,
Racine, Wisconsin 53404

14650-00

ISBN 0-307-14650-2

0 33500 14650 3

We'd be happy to answer your questions and hear your comments.

1-888-READ-2-ME

TOLL-FREE • United States Only
1-888-732-3263, 8 AM-10 PM EST, WEEKDAYS